ISBN:978-1-971933-37-5

Paperback Version

Printed in the United States of America

Published by Freshwater Press, 2026

Table of Contents

INTRO 5

RESPECT 11

Respect Is the First Green Flag 12

COMMUNICATION 19

Communication That Feels Safe 20

CONSISTENCY 28

CONSISTENCY IS GREATER THAN CHEMISTRY 29

EMOTIONAL MATURITY 37

EMOTIONAL MATURITY IS ATTRACTIVE 38

CHARACTER 45

CHARACTER OVER AESTHETICS 46

SOCIAL MEDIA 54

SOCIAL MEDIA REVEALS THE TRUTH 55

CONFLICT 63

CONFLICT SHOWS YOU WHO THEY REALLY ARE 64

PACE & PRESSURE 71

IF THEY RUSH YOU, THEY'RE NOT READY 72

DIRECTION 79

Direction Matters More Than Potential..80

BECOME THE GREEN FLAG 87

When There Are Too Many People in the Relationship 88

BECOME THE GREEN FLAG 95

CHOOSE WITH THE FUTURE IN MIND 104

Appendix A : Master List of 100 Green Flags: 105

Other Relationship Books.................................... 113

100 GREEN FLAGS:

DATE THIS NOT THAT

How to spot a good guy or a good girl

by Dr. Marlene Miles

INTRO

Hey, is that a Green Flag?

Most bad relationships don't start bad. They start exciting. Someone is funny. Someone texts you all the time. Someone says you're different from everyone else.

And at first, it feels good.

But then little things start happening. Red flags start popping up.

They interrupt you when you talk. They tease you in ways that make you uncomfortable. They ignore your "no" and act like you're being dramatic.

You tell yourself it's not a big deal.

But those little things are not random. They're signals. Most people know how to spot red flags — the warning signs. We have to learn how to spot and recognize green flags.

Green flags are the behaviors that show someone is emotionally healthy, respectful, and capable of a good relationship.

This book is about learning to recognize those signs early — so you can choose people who bring peace instead of problems.

What Is a Green Flag?

You've probably heard people talk about red flags. A red flag is a warning sign. It's behavior that tells you that something here is not healthy.

A green flag is the opposite.

A green flag is a good sign about someone's character. It's behavior that shows you a person is respectful, decent and:

- emotionally healthy
- trustworthy
- capable of a good relationship

Think of it like traffic lights.

● Red flag: Stop. Something is wrong.

● Yellow flag: Slow down. Pay attention.

● Green flag: This is a good sign. Keep going.

A green flag doesn't mean someone is perfect. No one is perfect, but it means they consistently show healthy behavior. They don't just use nice words, but it is their behavior that tells the truth in relationships.

Jordan & Tasha

Jordan liked how funny and charming Tasha was, but she noticed something small: He was only nice when *he wanted something*. He'd talk sweet to her and then turn around and be rude to the waiter. He'd laugh at her boundaries, ignore her when she said, "I'm not comfortable," and call her "dramatic" for speaking up. She finally realized that he didn't respect her. He just wanted **access**. Once she stopped ignoring the disrespect, she saw the truth: his kindness was conditional, but his ego was permanent.

If you say, "I don't like when you joke about that." A respectful person says: "Got it. I won't do it again." A disrespectful person says: "You're too sensitive. Lighten up." One is safe. The other is dangerous long-term unless they change. Grown people don't often or readily change.

When she was 20, Tasha thought Jordan's sarcasm was playful and his mood swings were "just his personality." She told herself, "It's not that deep — we're young."

Fast Forward — age 35:

She's now divorced with a 7-year-old. Tasha is in therapy for emotional exhaustion. She is shocked that the same things she *ignored at 20* became the same things that *broke the marriage at 32*.

Lesson:

Red flags don't fade — they multiply.

Green flags point the right way.

Anyone can say they care. Green flags show you how someone actually treats people. The earlier you learn to recognize them, the easier it becomes to choose people who bring peace instead of problems.

A green flag is a behavior that shows someone is a good person to date. They may not be perfect, but at least they are respectful. Remember dating is for the purpose of seeing who you may want to marry. Dating is not just for entertainment or just to have something to do. Dating is also not for the *other person's* entertainment; that is not your job.

A green flag means that you feel safe, valued, and respected around this person. You don't feel conflicted or confused. You don't feel pressured or constantly stressed.

Good relationships don't start with drama. They start with green flags. Love shouldn't feel like guessing or anxiety.

Bare minimum decent behavior is **not** a green flag, it is just the bare minimum for a human being.

This book is about what you may have not been taught about respect, peace, and emotional safety. If no one ever modeled healthy love for you, this book will

***A Note About the Workbook**

This book explains the green flags that help you recognize healthy relationships.

If you want to apply these ideas more personally, there is also a companion workbook designed to go with this book.

The **100 Green Flags Workbook** includes reflection questions, checklists, and exercises to help you think through your own experiences and relationship patterns.

You do not need the workbook to benefit from this book, but some readers find it helpful when they want to explore the ideas more deeply.

RESPECT

1. **Listens without interrupting.**
2. **Respects your "no" the first time.**
3. **Doesn't joke at your expense.**
4. **Speaks respectfully even when upset.**
5. **Treats you the same in public and in private.**
6. **Doesn't pressure your boundaries.**
7. **Doesn't flirt to make you insecure.**
8. **Values your opinions.**
9. **Doesn't compete with your confidence.**
10. **Treats everyone with dignity, not just you.**

CHAPTER 1

Respect Is the First Green Flag

If they don't respect you, nothing else matters.

There are people who will say they like you. There are people who will say they love you. Respect is what proves how they really feel about you.

You can survive without chemistry. You can survive without constant texting. You can survive without grand romantic gestures. You cannot build anything stable without respect.

Here is the problem most young people face: Disrespect.

Disrespect does not always arrive loudly. Sometimes it arrives joking. Sometimes it arrives charming. Sometimes it arrives wrapped in confidence. Whatever it's wrapped in, that's a disguise.

It looks small at first. An eye roll. They say, "You're too sensitive." A joke about your body. A sarcastic comment in front of friends.

Ignoring your *No* and asking again for something you already said, *No* to.

Those seem like tiny cracks. But cracks don't stay tiny. They expand under pressure.

A respectful person:

- Listens when you speak (not waiting to reply, but to really hear you and understand)
- Doesn't joke at your expense
- Respects your boundaries the *first time*
- Doesn't treat you like an option while expecting loyalty
- Doesn't flirt with others to make you insecure

Maya thought teasing was flirting — until she realized it was **disrespect**.

Before love, before attraction, before commitment — there has to be **respect**. You can't build a healthy relationship with someone who likes your face but doesn't value your voice, time, boundaries, or emotions. A person who truly respects you doesn't make you earn it, they show it from the beginning.

Respect shows up in pace: "I like you, but I won't rush you."

Respect Actually Looks Like:

Respect is not fear.
Respect is not obsession.
Respect is not possessiveness.

Respect means:

- They listen when you speak.
- They accept your boundaries without negotiation.
- They do not embarrass you for entertainment.
- They treat you consistently in public and private.
- They speak to you with dignity, even when irritated.

Respect is steady. It does not fluctuate with mood. Don't **miss this b**ecause disrespect is often disguised as:

- "He's just blunt."
- "She's just passionate."
- "That's just his personality."
- "You know how she is."

But here's the truth: If someone can choose and control how they speak to their boss, they can control how they speak to you.

Disrespect is not lack of control. It is lack of regard.

Tiana (Girl's POV)

At 19:

Tiana thought sarcasm meant chemistry.

He teased her in front of friends.
He called her dramatic when she expressed discomfort.
He told her she was "lucky" he liked her.

She laughed it off. She didn't know she was slowly shrinking.

Marcus (Guy's POV)

At 21:

Marcus liked how bold she was. But when he said no to something physical, she mocked him.
When he asked for space, she accused him of not being "man enough."

He stayed longer than he should have, because he thought endurance meant maturity.

It didn't.

FAST FORWARD — Age 35

Tiana is now divorced and relearning how to speak without apologizing.

Marcus is married to a woman who respects his voice — and he says the biggest relief in his life is not being mocked for having boundaries.

Disrespect ignored at 20 becomes erosion at 35.

The Truth

If someone cannot respect you while dating, they will not respect you in marriage. Marriage magnifies everything.

Respect is not the bonus. It is the foundation.

Date This / Not That

✅ "I didn't mean to hurt you. I'll fix that."

❌ "You're too sensitive."

✅ Lets you finish speaking and actually listens.

❌ Interrupts you when you're explaining something.

✅ Protects your dignity, even when joking.

✗ Makes jokes that embarrass you.

10 GREEN FLAGS OF REAL RESPECT

1. They listen when you speak — not just wait to talk.

Good sign: They respond to what you *actually* said, not what they assume. Bad sign: They interrupt, talk over you, or make everything about them.

2. They respect your "no" without giving you attitude.

A boundary isn't a challenge — it's information. A good person accepts it the first time.

3. They don't joke at your expense.

Teasing that embarrasses you is not "flirting." It's disrespect in a hoodie.

4. They don't treat you like an option while expecting loyalty from you.

If you're not exclusive, then they don't get exclusive benefits. Period.

5. They don't downplay your dreams or goals.

Someone who sees your ambition as a threat is not a partner; they're a competitor.

6. They don't use "that's just how I am" to excuse rude behavior.

Self-awareness without self-correction is manipulation.

7. They don't talk to you crazy and apologize with "but I was mad."

Disrespect is not a mood swing. It's a character leak.

8. They treat waiters, janitors, Uber drivers, and teachers with the same tone they use with you.

If they only respect people they want something from, that's not respect — that's strategy.

9. They don't make you feel small so they can feel big.

A good person will uplift you, not compete with you for confidence.

11. **They don't pressure you to move faster than you're ready for.**

REFLECTION

When you think about your last relationship,
did you feel valued — or managed?

COMMUNICATION

11. **Says what they mean clearly.**
12. **Doesn't disappear without explanation.**
13. **Can apologize without blaming you.**
14. **Doesn't mock your feelings.**
15. **Clarifies misunderstandings calmly.**
16. **Doesn't expect mind-reading.**
17. **Can handle hard conversations.**
18. **Keeps tone respectful during disagreement.**
19. **Doesn't gaslight or minimize concerns.**
20. **Makes you feel calm, not anxious.**

CHAPTER 2

Communication That Feels Safe

No games. No confusion. No mixed signals.

A healthy relationship never makes you feel like you're decoding a mystery. When someone is good for you, the communication feels clear, calm, and consistent — not like a scavenger hunt for "what they *really* meant."

If you have to *overthink*, *translate*, *chase*, or "read between the lines," that's not love — that's emotional instability disguised as chemistry.

Good communication isn't perfect.
It's honest + steady + respectful.
And most of all: it makes you feel safe, not anxious.

There is a difference between talking and communicating.

Some people talk constantly. They text all day. They send memes. They flirt. They joke. And yet you still feel confused.

Communication is not volume; it is clarity. A healthy relationship should not feel like decoding a puzzle.

You should not have to guess:

- Are we okay?
- Are they mad?
- Are we exclusive?
- Are they serious?
- Did I do something wrong?

If love feels like anxiety, something is off.

Kayla (Girl's POV)

At 19:

Kayla liked that Malik was funny and charismatic — but every time she asked a real question, he'd either joke, dodge, or get irritated. If she asked, "Where is this going?" he'd reply, "Why you always need a title?"

If she said, "That hurt my feelings," he'd say, "You're too emotional."

She didn't realize it yet, but she was being trained to **stop expressing her feelings** just to "keep the peace."

Devon (Guy's POV)

At 20:

Devon liked how smart and beautiful Aria was, but when she got upset, she wouldn't talk — she'd block him, disappear, then come back like nothing happened.

She'd say, "Communication is important," but her actions were chaos. He always felt like he was about to be cut off for something he didn't know he did.

He finally realized: **communication isn't just talking — it's accountability, too.**

FAST FORWARD (Age 33)

Kayla is now divorced with a 5-year-old and sitting in a counselor's office, trying to *re-learn* how to express her needs without fear.

Devon is in a relationship with a woman who communicates with honesty and grace — and he now understands that **peace is priceless**.

Both of them learned the same lesson: **Confusing communication at 21 turns into emotional exhaustion at 35.**

What Safe Communication Actually Feels Like

Safe communication feels steady. It does not mean constant contact. It means predictable honesty. It looks like:

- "I need space tonight, but we're good."
- "That hurt my feelings. Can we talk?"
- "I was wrong."
- "I misunderstood you."
- "Let's fix this."

Notice something:
None of those statements are dramatic.

Healthy communication is not intense.
It is responsible.

Why Confusing Communication Hooks People

Unpredictable communication creates anxiety. And anxiety creates attachment.

When someone is warm one day and cold the next, your brain tries to "solve" them.

That chase feels like passion. It isn't. It's emotional instability creating a reward cycle.

If someone disappears for two days and then returns affectionate, your nervous system feels relief. That relief can feel like love. It's not. It's the end of stress.

Healthy communication does not make you oscillate between panic and peace. Healthy communication keeps you steady.

The Truth

If someone refuses to clarify,
refuses to apologize,
refuses to explain,
refuses to engage in hard conversations— They are not protecting peace. They are protecting control.

Communication is not about winning. It is about building trust. And trust cannot grow where clarity is avoided.

DATE THIS, NOT THAT

✅ **Date This:** *"If something feels unclear, just ask. I don't want you guessing."* (Translation: *I want a real relationship, not a power dynamic.*)

❌ **Not That:** *"You're overthinking. I don't like explaining myself."* (Translation: *I want access without responsibility.*)

DATE THIS, NOT THAT

✅ "Hey, I needed space earlier, but I'm back. Can we talk tonight?"

❌ "Sorry I disappeared, I was just in a mood."

DATE THIS, NOT THAT

✅ **Date This:**
- "I may not reply fast, but I won't disappear."
- "I want to be dependable — not just romantic."
- "If something changes, I'll tell you before you worry."

❌ **Not That:**
- "I've just been busy."
- "You know how I get sometimes."
- "Why do you need me to say everything?"

10 GREEN FLAGS IN COMMUNICATION

1. They say what they mean — no "guess what I'm thinking" games.

You don't have to be a mind-reader to be with them.

2. They don't go missing for days and call it "space."

Healthy people don't disappear — they communicate.

3. They don't punish you with silence.

Disagreement isn't a reason to shut down or go ghost.

4. They answer questions without making you feel dumb for asking.

If you have to apologize for needing clarity, something's off.

5. They correct misunderstandings instead of letting you panic.

A good person reassures you, not confuses you.

6. They can say "I was wrong" without collapsing.

Accountability is not a sign of weakness — it's maturity.

7. They don't turn every conversation into a debate or a win/lose battle.

Healthy people talk to understand — not to dominate.

8. Their tone matches their words.

"I'm not mad" — *in a mad tone* — is emotional dishonesty.

9. They don't mock your feelings, even if they don't agree.

Emotional safety > always being right.

10. They don't avoid hard conversations — they handle them with care.

Silence and avoidance kill more relationships than arguments ever will.

REFLECTION

When you think about your current or last relationship, did you feel calm most of the time?

CONSISTENCY

21. **Follows through on promises.**
22. **Shows up when they say they will.**
23. **Doesn't love-bomb then withdraw.**
24. **Is steady over time.**
25. **Doesn't "switch up" after getting comfortable.**
26. **Doesn't only show effort when losing access.**
27. **Doesn't punish with silence.**
28. **Is reliable with time and plans.**
29. **Doesn't make you compete for attention.**
30. **Cares consistently, not conditionally.**

CHAPTER 3

CONSISTENCY IS GREATER THAN CHEMISTRY

Someone who is steady beats someone who is exciting-but-chaotic.

Chemistry can make you *feel* connected, but consistency proves whether the connection is real. It's easy to be charming for a week. It's easy to be sweet when they want something. It's easy to act right in the beginning.

Consistency is character in motion.

Real green flag behavior doesn't come and go — it *stays.*

A good partner isn't perfect every day, but they're **predictable in the best way**. You don't have to guess which version of them you're getting today.

Chemistry feels exciting.

R**omantic sparks are easy.**

Emotional steadiness is rare.

Consistency feels safe.

Most young people choose excitement. Later, they wish they had chosen safety.

Chemistry is immediate.
Consistency is proven.

Chemistry says, “I’ve never felt this before.”

Consistency says, “You can depend on me.”

One feels like fireworks. The other feels like foundation. Fireworks are beautiful, but you cannot live inside them.

Inconsistency Feels Addictive

When someone is hot and cold, your brain releases a hormone called dopamine.

The unpredictability creates intensity; you release more dopamine.

You begin to crave their attention because you never know when you’ll get it. The brain confuses unpredictability with importance.

That is why someone who texts nonstop for three days and then disappears can feel unforgettable. Not because they are healthy; they are not. They are unstable.

- The same in public, private, and online
- Doesn't "switch up" after getting what they want
- Shows up when they said they would
- Doesn't use silence or distance to punish
- Isn't perfect — just dependable

Zay was charming... until she realized she never knew which version of him was showing up, or if he was showing up at all.

JANELLE & LEO (Girl's POV)

At 18:

Janelle loved how romantic Leo was — flowers, surprises, long calls, the whole movie script.

But every time she got comfortable, he'd pull away. He'd say things like, "I just need time," then pop back in like nothing happened.

She kept thinking, *"If I'm more patient, maybe he'll stay."* She didn't know yet that she was stuck in a cycle: **love-bomb → neglect → apology → repeat.**

CHADWICK & ALINA (Guy's POV)

At 22:

Chadwick thought Alina was "different" from the girls he'd dated — she was smart, beautiful, and spiritual.

But she was loyal only when it was convenient.
One minute, she wanted a future.
The next, she was "confused" and wanted to "just talk to other people."

He finally realized something: **It wasn't that she didn't know what she wanted — she just didn't want *him* consistently.**

FAST FORWARD (Age 34)

Janelle now has two kids and tells her therapist she always feels like she's "trying to earn love."

Chadwick is now engaged to a woman whose love is steady — not dramatic. He says the biggest relief in his life is "knowing she won't switch up tomorrow."

Leo is still playing the field and his ankles are dusty from being out there so long.

You don't fix inconsistency. You just stop accepting it.

DATE THIS, NOT THAT

✅ **Date This:**
"Something came up tonight, but I want to reschedule."
And they actually follow through.
(Translation: When I say you matter, my actions make room for you.)

❌ **Not That:**
"Sorry, my mom needed me... my kid needed me... my friend needed me." *(again)*
Plans constantly fall apart because someone "needed them."
(Translation: I keep you on standby while something else is always the priority.)

✅ **Date This:**
"I've been busy, but I still want to make time for you. Let's plan something."

❌ **Not That:**
"I just get busy sometimes. You know how I am."
(Translation: I show up when it's convenient for me, not when it matters to you.)

✅ **Date This:**
"I couldn't answer earlier, but I didn't want to leave you wondering."

❌ **Not That:**
"I didn't text back because I figured you'd understand."
(Translation: Your time and feelings are optional to me.)

10 GREEN FLAGS OF CONSISTENCY

1. Their actions match their words — repeatedly.

Promises aren't impressive. Follow-through is.

2. They don't "switch up" once they feel secure.

The person they were while getting you is the same person while keeping you.

3. They don't give you 10/10 effort one week and vanish the next.

You shouldn't have to "earn" their good behavior.

4. They don't treat you better when they're guilty or losing access.

Consistency isn't just during the honeymoon phase — it's during conflict too.

5. They're not affectionate only when they want something.

If love is tied to benefit, it's not love — it's a transaction.

6. They are reliable with time, communication, and follow-through.

Unreliability is a personality trait, not an accident.

7. They don't flirt with stability but date like chaos.

What they say they want matches how they behave.

8. They don't blame "mood swings" for treating you differently.

Moodiness is not a moral Get Out of Jail Free card.

9. You don't feel like you're auditioning for a spot in their life.

A consistent person gives security, not competition.

10. They don't need to be reminded how to care about you.

Real effort is self-initiated, not supervised.

What Consistency Actually Looks Like

Consistency means:

- They show up when they say they will.
- Their tone does not radically shift.
- They don't love-bomb and then withdraw.
- They don't punish you with distance.
- They are the same in private and public.

Consistency is boring to people addicted to chaos. Consistency builds marriages.

REFLECTION

"Have I ever confused inconsistency with passion?"

EMOTIONAL MATURITY

31. **Owns mistakes without excuses.**
32. **Regulates anger.**
33. **Doesn't threaten breakup during conflict.**
34. **Doesn't guilt-trip.**
35. **Doesn't weaponize trauma.**
36. **Takes responsibility for growth.**
37. **Doesn't blame their past for bad behavior.**
38. **Can disagree respectfully.**
39. **Handles stress without lashing out.**
40. **Values growth over ego.**

CHAPTER 4

EMOTIONAL MATURITY IS ATTRACTIVE

Can they handle life without making you responsible for their meltdown?

Anyone can *want* a relationship. Not everyone is emotionally mature enough to handle one.

Emotional maturity shows up in the way someone deals with:

- Disappointment
- Disagreement
- Stress
- Boundaries
- Not getting their way

A person who is not emotionally mature will turn their feelings into your responsibility. A person who *is* emotionally mature will feel their feelings without destroying the relationship.

The right person won't always be calm — but they'll always be accountable. The right one:

- Can apologize without blaming
- Takes accountability without "BUT YOU..."
- Doesn't turn every disagreement into a breakup threat
- Handles stress without destroying people
- Knows love ≠ ownership

Scenario: "You said, No. Did they respect it or guilt-trip you?"

Emotional Immaturity can look like:

• Passion.
• Trauma depth.
• Intensity.
• "I just love hard."

But it's none of those things.

Here's the truth: If someone cannot regulate their emotions, you will become the regulator. And that is exhausting.

Serena (Girl's POV)

At 20:

Serena thought Andre was deep because he talked about trauma, depression, "trust issues," and needing a "different kind of love."

But whenever she felt hurt and tried to talk about it, he'd explode, cry, or shut down. She mistook **emotional chaos for emotional depth**. She thought being "understanding" meant staying quiet so she didn't trigger him.

She didn't know yet: **you can't love someone into maturity.**

Elijah (Male's POV)

At 21:

Elijah thought Serena was "real" because she was bold and unfiltered. But every time he tried to have a grown conversation, she'd mock him or say, "Why are you so sensitive?" If he set a boundary, she'd say, "Wow, you're controlling now?"

He finally got it—someone who acts super confident can actually be immature, and you don't realize it until they have to own up to their mistakes.

FAST FORWARD (Age 32)

Serena is now a woman who has spent thousands in therapy learning how to speak without apologizing for having feelings.

Elijah is now dating someone who can disagree without destroying connection — and he finally understands that *peace is not the same as "boring."*

Both of them now know:

You don't outgrow emotional immaturity — you drown in it, or walk away from it.

DATE THIS, NOT THAT

✅ **Date This:**
"I got frustrated, but that's no excuse. I'll work on how I react next time."
(Translation: *I'm responsible for my behavior, even when emotional.*)

❌ **Not That:**
"I only act like that because I love hard."
(Translation: *I refuse to control myself, so you have to adjust.*)

☑ **Date This:**
"I was upset, but I still should've handled that better."
(Translation: My emotions are my responsibility.)

✕ **Not That:**
"You made me act like that."
(Translation: I blame you for my behavior instead of controlling myself.)

☑ **Date This:**
"I need a minute to cool down before we talk about this."
(Translation: I'm responsible for regulating my emotions.)

✕ **Not That:**
"If you really loved me, you wouldn't make me mad."
(Translation: I expect you to manage my feelings for me.)

The Truth

Love does not fix immaturity. Time does not fix immaturity; only growth does. If someone is not committed to growth, they are not ready for commitment. *Being in a relationship doesn't make someone mature. Handling emotions well does.*

10 GREEN FLAGS OF EMOTIONAL MATURITY

1. They can apologize without blaming you for their behavior.

"Sorry, *but you made me mad*" is not an apology.

2. They can stay respectful even when they're upset.

Anger is a feeling. Disrespect is a choice.

3. They don't use threats, guilt, or silence to control you.

Emotional punishment is abuse with a soft voice.

4. They don't act like the whole world is against them.

Victim mentality = zero accountability.

5. They don't expect you to "fix" them.

If love feels like therapy, you're not their partner — you're their coping mechanism.

6. They don't turn every disagreement into a breakup or a meltdown.

Immature people need drama to feel powerful.

7. They don't blame their past for present bad behavior.

Healing may explain, but it does not excuse.

8. They can talk about feelings *without exploding or shutting down.*

Healthy communication is not a personality type — it's a skill.

9. They don't confuse honesty with cruelty.

"You're too sensitive" = emotional laziness, not truth.

10. They want growth, not comfort that protects their flaws.

Mature people don't fear accountability — they value it.

REFLECTION

When conflict happens, do you feel safe? Or do you brace yourself? Be honest.

CHARACTER

41. Is honest even when it costs them.

42. Keeps promises.

43. Shows humility.

44. Speaks well of others.

45. Doesn't gossip excessively.

46. Respects people who can't benefit them.

47. Doesn't brag about basic decency.

48. Celebrates your wins.

49. Has integrity when unobserved.

50. Doesn't manipulate to get their way.

CHAPTER 5

CHARACTER OVER AESTHETICS

Cute, funny, and popular are not personality traits. Only character ages well.

At 16, 18, 22 — it's easy to think the most important thing is who you're *attracted* to. But attraction will get you interested. **Character is what keeps you safe.**

The person who looks good in pictures may not look good in your *future*. Pretty eyes, nice smile, good hair, nice body, great style, popular, "everybody wants them" — cool. But here's the truth no one tells young people:

Cute won't matter when they're yelling at you.
Handsome won't matter when they're lying to you.
Beauty won't matter when you can't trust them.

And yet... Kindness? Loyalty? Humility? Integrity? Those age like gold.

- Treats the waiter or janitor the same as you
- Has friends who respect them
- Doesn't need an audience to act right
- Is proud of you, not competitive with you
- Keeps promises even when no one is watching

Attraction is powerful. But attraction is not character. Someone can look good, dress well, have perfect hair, be funny, popular, charming, and still lack integrity.

And integrity is what you will live with.

Looks fade. Style changes. Bodies age. Character deepens — or exposes itself.

The mistake many young people make is believing that attraction equals compatibility. It doesn't. Attraction gets you interested. Character determines whether you are safe.

What Character Actually Looks Like

Character is revealed in small, everyday moments.

• How they treat people who cannot benefit them
• How they speak about others when they are not present

• Whether they keep promises when no one is watching
• Whether they tell the truth when lying would be easier
• Whether they are humble enough to grow

Character is not performance.

It is consistency when the spotlight is off.

Mini-Story: “He was fine, but she realized he had no integrity.”

Leah (Girl’s POV)

At 17:

Leah was obsessed with how perfect Jay looked — waves, shoes always clean, gym body, social media popping.

But his kindness had conditions. He was rude to waiters, trashed people behind their backs, and loved being “above” everybody.

She ignored the signs because *“he’s just confident.”* She didn’t know yet, but **ego ages badly. Very badly.**

Chris (Guy's POV)

At 23:

Chris thought Bri was "rare" — gorgeous, popular, always dressed like she was going somewhere elite.

But she dismissed people she thought were "beneath her." If someone didn't benefit her, she didn't see them. She spoke with entitlement, not kindness.

He eventually learned: **Beauty without humility becomes disrespect in a relationship.**

FAST FORWARD (Age 35)

Leah is now co-parenting with a man who still thinks the world revolves around him. He posts more than he parents.

Chris is now married to a woman who isn't "the most followed," but she is the most emotionally safe person he's ever known. He would never trade peace for popularity again.

Popularity fades. Character echoes.

DATE THIS, NOT THAT (Example)

✅ **Date This:**
"I try to treat everyone with respect, no matter their status."
(Translation: My values don't change depending on the audience.)

❌ **Not That:**
"I don't really mess with people who can't do something for me."
(Translation: My relationships are transactional.)

✅ **Date This:**
"I should've told the truth. That's on me."
(Translation: My integrity matters even when it's uncomfortable.)

❌ **Not That:**
"I only lied because it wasn't a big deal."
(Translation: I decide when honesty matters.)

✅ **Date This:**
"I was angry, but that doesn't mean I should treat someone badly."
(Translation: My character doesn't disappear when I'm mad.)

❌ **Not That:**
"They deserved it."
(Translation: I justify hurting people if I'm upset.)

The Truth

Do not let someone's aesthetic blind you to their ethic.

Pretty without principles becomes pain.

Handsome without humility becomes harm.

Choose character.

Why Appearance Distracts Us

At 16, 18, 22 — social status feels powerful. If someone is admired, followed, desired, or considered "out of your league," it feels validating to be chosen. But validation is not stability.

Being chosen by someone *impressive* does not mean they are good for you.

The question is not: "Do people want them?"

The question is: "Are they trustworthy?"

10 GREEN FLAGS OF CHARACTER

1. They treat people *with no status* the same as people with status.

How they treat a stranger says more than how they treat you.

2. They don't brag about doing the bare minimum.

If they flex "I don't cheat," the bar is in the dirt.

3. They're honest even when dishonesty would benefit them.

Character shows when no one's watching.

4. They don't need attention to feel valuable.

People who are full don't hunger for validation.

5. They don't embarrass you for entertainment.

A person who loves you won't use you as content.

6. They don't get jealous of your wins.

A real partner celebrates you — doesn't compete with you.

7. They don't use cheating, lying, ghosting, or blocking as "normal parts of dating."

Respect is not a personality type. It's a standard.

8. They are kind to people who can't do anything for them.

Empathy is not selective — it's rooted.

9. They don't see "loyalty" as ownership or control.

Healthy people want partnership, not possession.

10. They want to grow — not just impress.

Pretty + unteachable = pain later.

REFLECTION PROMPT:

If their looks disappeared, would I still want this person?

SOCIAL MEDIA

51. **Online behavior matches real-life values.**
52. **Doesn't act single online.**
53. **Doesn't entertain flirtatious comments.**
54. **Doesn't hide you to appear available.**
55. **Doesn't DM others secretly.**
56. **Doesn't subtweet you.**
57. **Doesn't seek validation excessively.**
58. **Doesn't embarrass exes publicly.**
59. **Is transparent about digital boundaries.**
60. **Protects your dignity online.**

CHAPTER 6

SOCIAL MEDIA REVEALS THE TRUTH

People show their values through their posts, likes, comments, and DMs.

You don't need a private investigator — just look at their online behavior. Social media is where people **reveal who they are when they think it doesn't count.**

Someone can say, "I'm loyal," but follow, like, and DM people in ways that prove the opposite.

Someone can say, "I respect you," but hide you online like you're a liability.

Someone can say, "I'm not messy," but post drama, shade, thirst traps, and seek attention 24/7.

Dating in the modern world requires **watching how they behave digitally, not just socially.**

Because here's the truth:

Your relationship shouldn't have to fight the internet.

We live in a digital world.

The internet does not create character; it reveals it.

Someone may speak about loyalty in person, but their likes, comments, follows, and DMs tell a different story.

Pay attention, because how someone behaves online often reflects what they believe doesn't "count."

What Healthy Digital Behavior Looks Like

Their online presence does not contradict their real-life commitments.

They do not flirt publicly while claiming exclusivity privately.

They do not hide you to appear available.

They do not entertain attention that disrespects the relationship.

They do not subtweet you instead of speaking to you.

Healthy people do not need an audience to validate loyalty.

Why This Matters So Much

Online behavior can seem harmless.

"It's just Instagram."
"It's just TikTok."
"It's just comments."

But attention feeds ego. And ego unchecked damages relationships.

If someone needs strangers to feel desirable, they will struggle to feel content with stability.

Autumn (Girl's POV)

At 18:

Autumn thought Jacari was "just social" because he was always commenting, always reacting, always in somebody's DMs with "You look gorgeous."

She told herself, *"He's just friendly."* But every time she asked about it, he'd say, "Relax, it's just Instagram."

She didn't realize yet:
If someone needs public attention to feel valuable, they'll always risk private trust.

Isaac (Guy's POV)

At 24:

Isaac loved how confident Ava was — selfies, reels, TikToks, always glowing. But every time he asked about exclusivity, she'd say, "I don't like labels, I'm just vibing."

Meanwhile, her comments were full of "You're so fine," "Marry me," and heart eyes — and she *never* corrected it.

He finally understood. She didn't want a partner. She wanted **an audience.**

FAST FORWARD (Age 33)

Autumn is now in a relationship where she doesn't have to compete with strangers online for her partner's attention.

Isaac now says the biggest peace in his life is not having to wonder what his woman is doing on the internet at 2 a.m.

Both of them learned:

The way someone handles attention online will either protect you — or humiliate you.

DATE THIS, NOT THAT (Online Edition)

✅ **Date This:**
Posts however they want — but nothing about their online behavior contradicts their loyalty.
(Translation: My public behavior matches my real-life commitment.)

❌ **Not That:**
Posts like they're single. DMs like they're single. Gets defensive when you ask about it.
(Translation: I want the benefits of a relationship and the attention of being single.)

✅ **Date This:**
"If something online makes you uncomfortable, let's talk about it."
(Translation: I care about trust more than attention.)

❌ **Not That:**
"It's just Instagram. Why are you making it a big deal?"

(Translation: I want to keep behavior online that I wouldn't defend in person.)

✅ **Date This:**
Has nothing to hide in their messages or interactions.
(Translation: Transparency is normal when you're loyal.)

❌ **Not That:**
Deletes messages or hides conversations when you walk in.
(Translation: I know this behavior crosses a line.)

The Truth

Your relationship should not have to compete with the internet.

If someone values you, their digital life will reflect it.

10 GREEN FLAGS IN SOCIAL MEDIA BEHAVIOR

1. They don't act single online while claiming you offline.

Nobody's asking for a 7-paragraph love post — just alignment.

2. They don't flirt in comments, likes, or DMs for attention.

"It's just social media" is gaslighting in a cute font.

3. They don't follow accounts only for bodies, thirst, or fantasy.

What they feed on is who they are becoming.

4. They don't delete messages or hide activity to protect their image.

Privacy is fine. Secrecy is not.

5. They don't use their story to subtweet you instead of talking to you.

Mature people don't post what they should discuss.

6. They don't "turn you invisible" online to keep options open.

If you're a secret, they're not committed — they're recruiting.

7. They have the same personality in person and online.

Double lives are easy to run on Wi-Fi.

8. They don't chase validation from strangers while ignoring your feelings.

Attention addiction destroys relationships one like at a time.

9. They don't mock, expose, or embarrass exes or friends online.

If they dishonor others publicly, your turn is coming.

10. They don't need to broadcast loyalty — they live it.

Silent respect > loud performance.

REFLECTION PROMPT

Does their online behavior make me feel secure — or anxious?

CONFLICT

61. Doesn't insult during arguments.
62. Doesn't raise voice to dominate.
63. Doesn't block or ghost as punishment.
64. Doesn't threaten to leave to gain control.
65. Seeks resolution, not victory.
66. Apologizes sincerely.
67. Doesn't bring up past issues to win.
68. Doesn't humiliate you publicly.
69. Communicates during cooling-off periods.
70. Makes you feel safe after conflict.

CHAPTER 7

CONFLICT SHOWS YOU WHO THEY REALLY ARE

Every relationship will have disagreements, but only **unhealthy relationships** turn disagreements into *fear, disrespect, control, or emotional damage.*

People show their real character when:

- They don't get their way
- They're embarrassed
- They feel misunderstood
- They're angry, tired, or triggered

A person who is good for you won't just love you when it's easy, they'll **treat you with dignity even when it's hard.**

If conflict feels like war, the relationship is not love — it's a battlefield disguised as romance.

What matters is how those disagreements are handled.

Conflict does not destroy relationships.

Disrespect during conflict does.

When someone is upset, embarrassed, or frustrated — their true character surfaces. Pay attention then.

Healthy Conflict Looks Like

- They do not insult you
- They do not threaten to leave every time something goes wrong
- They do not weaponize silence
- They do not humiliate you publicly
- They do not escalate to dominate

Conflict should feel like resolution in progress — not emotional warfare.

Nyla (Girl's POV)

At 21:

Nyla thought Dre was just "passionate" because every disagreement turned into shouting, pacing, slamming doors. He always said, "I just talk loud — that's how I am."

But she noticed something: He never talked to his boss like that. Never talked to his boys like that. Just *her*.

She finally realized: **It wasn't a communication style — it was entitlement.**

Eli (Guy's POV)

At 19:

Eli thought Kira was "just emotional" when she gave him silent treatment for 3 days anytime she didn't get her way. No explanation. No conversation. Just coldness.

Then she'd come back like nothing happened and say, "I just needed time to think."

He learned the hard way: **Silent treatment isn't peace — it's punishment.**

FAST FORWARD (Age 32)

Nyla is now co-parenting with a man who still yells to feel powerful. Her daughter now flinches when voices rise — because kids don't copy words, they copy patterns.

Eli is now dating a woman who talks *through* conflict, not *around* it. He says the best feeling in the world is knowing disagreement doesn't equal destruction.

You can't build a peaceful life with someone who only knows war.

DATE THIS, NOT THAT

✅ **Date This:**

"I need 30 minutes to cool down, but I'm not going anywhere. Let's finish talking after." *(Translation: I handle conflict without abandoning the relationship.)*

❌ **Not That:**

"You're trippin'. I don't have time for this." *(hangs up)*. Threatens breakup, blocks, or disappears during arguments.
(Translation: I avoid problems by abandoning the conversation.)

✅ **Date This:**

"I didn't like what happened earlier. Can we talk about it?"
(Translation: I focus on the issue, not attacking you.)

✕ **Not That:**

"You always do this. You're impossible to deal with."
(Translation: I attack your character instead of solving the problem.)

☑ **Date This:**

"Let's stay on this issue and figure it out."
(Translation: Solving the problem matters more than being right.)

✕ **Not That:**

Brings up five old arguments to win the current one.
(Translation: I care more about winning than resolving the problem.)

The Truth

If someone cannot disagree respectfully, they are not ready to build anything long-term.

Love is not measured by intensity during arguments. It is measured by safety.

10 GREEN FLAGS IN HOW THEY HANDLE CONFLICT

1. They don't insult you, even when they're angry.

Anger explains tone — not cruelty.

2. They don't block, ghost, or disappear to "win."

Silence is not resolution — it's manipulation.

3. They take time to cool off without shutting you out.

Space is okay. Punishment is not.

4. They don't threaten to leave every time something goes wrong.

"Breakup threats" are emotional blackmail.

5. They don't get louder just to dominate.

Volume doesn't equal valid.

6. They care more about understanding than "winning."

Healthy people fight for the relationship — not for ego.

7. They don't bring up old things to stack guilt against you.

Recycled arguments = stored resentment.

8. They apologize without flipping the blame back on you.

"Sorry *you feel that way*" = not an apology.

9. They don't post about the argument online.

Real adults don't turn private problems into public entertainment.

10. They want resolution, not revenge.

Some people want peace. Some want power. Know the difference.

REFLECTION PROMPT

"Do I feel safe to tell them I'm hurt — or do I walk on eggshells?"

PACE & PRESSURE

71. **Moves at a healthy pace.**
72. **Doesn't rush exclusivity.**
73. **Doesn't rush physical intimacy.**
74. **Doesn't isolate you from friends/family.**
75. **Doesn't pressure long-term decisions quickly.**
76. **Builds trust before labels.**
77. **Is patient with your comfort level.**
78. **Doesn't guilt you for boundaries.**
79. **Doesn't love-bomb to secure loyalty.**
80. **Lets the relationship develop naturally.**

CHAPTER 8

IF THEY RUSH YOU, THEY'RE NOT READY

Some people will hurry you into a relationship because they're excited. Others will hurry you because they want control, access, or validation.

Attention is not the same as intention. Speed is not the same as sincerity. Intensity is not the same as stability.

Real love doesn't rush. It builds. If someone says, "I've never felt this way before" in week 2 but disappears when you set a boundary in week 3... That wasn't love — that was *urgency disguised as romance.*

Fast does not mean serious. Intensity does not mean maturity. And urgency does not mean destiny. When someone rushes a relationship, it can feel flattering.

"You're different."
"I've never felt this way."
"I see my future with you."
"Let's make this official right now."

Speed is not proof of stability. Sometimes it's proof of insecurity.

Why Rushing Feels Romantic

When someone moves quickly, it creates emotional momentum.

You feel chosen. Prioritized. Special.

But here is the question:

Do they want you? Or do they want the feeling of having you?

There is a difference.

People who rush often fear losing control.

They want access before accountability. Closeness before trust. Exclusivity before clarity.

Healthy love does not panic; it builds.

Lani & Chris (Girl's POV)

At 18:

Lani met Chris in April. By May, he was saying "You're my world." By June, he wanted to move in. By July, he was upset that she still wanted time with friends.

At first she thought, *"Wow, he's so serious about me."*

Then she realized: **He wasn't serious about *her* — he was serious about *owning her*. Speed was his strategy.**

Zac & Aliyah (Guy's POV)

At 23:

Zac met Aliyah, and within two weeks she was calling him "my man" on Instagram, buying matching hoodies, and tagging him in "future husband" posts.

When Zac said, "Let's slow down and get to know each other first," she got offended and posted,

"Some people don't know a good woman when they see her."

He learned:
Some people want the title, not the responsibility.
Some want the fantasy, not the work.

FAST FORWARD (Age 34)

Lani now understands that "too fast" always becomes "too much." She's raising a child with a man who rushes into everything — including new relationships.

Zac now says the healthiest love he's experienced didn't come with pressure. The right woman didn't rush him — she built *with* him.

Love that's real will wait for readiness.
Love that's insecure needs urgency.

DATE THIS, NOT THAT

❌ **Not That:**
"We don't need labels. I just want you to stop talking to other people."
(Translation: I want control without commitment.)

✅ **Date This:**
"I'm interested in something real, but let's take time to see if we're compatible."
(Translation: Real relationships build trust before exclusivity

---

✅ **Date This:**
"We don't have to rush anything. I want us both to feel comfortable."
(Translation: Respecting your pace matters more than forcing closeness.)

❌ **Not That:**
"Why are you taking this so slow? If you liked

me, you'd prove it."
(Translation: I want you to ignore your boundaries to make me feel secure.)

✅ **Date This:**
Lets the relationship develop naturally over time.
(Translation: Real connection grows — it isn't forced.)

❌ **Not That:**
Pushes emotional or physical closeness very quickly.
(Translation: I'm creating intensity before trust exists.)

What Healthy Pace Looks Like

- They take time to know your values.
- They respect your boundaries without guilt.
- They don't isolate you from friends or family.
- They don't push physical intimacy as proof of connection.
- They let trust grow naturally.

They are not in a race; they are in a relationship.

The Truth

If someone cannot build slowly, they cannot build securely. Love that is real does not require panic. It requires readiness.

10 GREEN FLAGS ABOUT PACE & PATIENCE

1. They don't push for commitment faster than trust is built.

If they want access before accountability — run.

2. They don't claim you without learning you.

"Let's be exclusive" requires maturity, not just butterflies.

3. They don't say "I love you" just to secure loyalty.

Words without foundation are emotional bait.

4. They don't try to isolate you from friends/family "quickly."

Speed + isolation = control.

5. They don't rush physical intimacy to create attachment.

If connection has to be *forced,* it's not real.

6. They don't future-talk ("kids, marriage, forever") while avoiding present growth.

Dreaming is easy. Discipline is harder.

7. They let the relationship breathe instead of suffocating it with pressure.

Healthy love has rhythm, not panic.

8. They don't guilt you for moving at a pace that feels safe.

Anyone bothered by your boundaries is planning to violate them.

9. They don't disappear when "fast" doesn't work — they adjust and stay.

Maturity stays. Immaturity sulks.

10. They're building something *with* you, not forcing something *out of* you.

Love invites. Control rushes.

REFLECTION PROMPT

"Do they want a *relationship* with me — or the *rush* of claiming me?"

DIRECTION

81. Has clear goals.
82. Works toward self-improvement.
83. Values stability.
84. Supports your ambitions.
85. Doesn't feel threatened by your success.
86. Makes responsible life decisions.
87. Has discipline.
88. Doesn't rely on fantasy plans.
89. Thinks long-term.
90. Wants partnership, not dependency.

CHAPTER 9

Direction Matters More Than Potential

Even if you're not ready for marriage yet — direction matters more than perfection.

You don't have to know who you'll marry at 17, 19, or 23 — but you *do* need to pay attention to whether the person you're dating is headed somewhere you can respect.

A relationship doesn't fail because someone didn't know everything about the future. It fails when **one person is building and the other is drifting.**

You don't need a perfect plan. You don't need a 5-year spreadsheet. But you *do* need someone who:

- Has goals
- Has values
- Has self-awareness
- Has a growth mindset
- Has something to lose if they mess up

Because here's the truth:

A futureless person will always be careless with your future too.

Potential is attractive. Direction is powerful. Many young people fall in love with who someone *could be*. But relationships are built with who someone currently **is**.

It is not your job to develop someone into maturity. It is your job to choose wisely.

Why Potential Is Misleading

Potential creates hope.

Hope creates patience.

Patience can turn into waiting.

Waiting can turn into wasted years.

If someone has no direction, no discipline, and no demonstrated growth — potential is a fantasy because fantasy cannot sustain partnership.

Sasha & Miles (Girl's POV)

At 19:

Sasha liked that Miles was chill, funny, and "in the moment." But every time she mentioned dreams — college, career, travel — he'd say, "Why you always stressing the future? We're young."

She kept trying to pull him into purpose... but he wasn't lost. He was *comfortable standing still.*

She didn't know yet: **If someone has no direction, love won't give them one.**

Andre & Tia (Guy's POV)

At 22:

Andre loved how confident Tia was, but anytime he mentioned building something long-term, she'd say, "I don't plan — I just manifest."

Meanwhile: no job plan, no money plan, no growth plan — but endless "one day I'll..." speeches. She liked the *idea* of the future... just not the *work* required to get there.

He learned: **Some people want success without strategy — and that becomes your burden if you stay.**

FAST FORWARD (Age 33)

Sasha is now a woman raising a child with a man who still has no direction — just older and still "figuring it out."

Andre is now engaged to a woman who doesn't need him to drag her into purpose — she already had her own, and now they build together.

The future you want needs a partner who's also preparing for theirs.

DATE THIS, NOT THAT (Future Example)

✅ **Date This:**

"I don't know every step yet, but I'm working toward something."
(Translation: I care about building a future, not just passing time.)

❌ **Not That:**

"I don't really think about the future. I just go with the flow."
(Translation: I drift instead of building.)

✅ **Date This:**

"I like that you have goals. What are you working toward?"
(Translation: I respect growth and direction.)

❌ **Not That:**

"Why are you always talking about goals? Just relax."
(Translation: Your ambition makes me uncomfortable.)

✅ **Date This:**

"I want to build a life I'm proud of."
(Translation: My choices today connect to my future.)

❌ **Not That:**

"I don't care what happens in five years. We're still young; what's the rush?"
(Translation: I'm not thinking long-term.)

10 GREEN FLAGS OF FUTURE ALIGNMENT

1. They have goals beyond "vibes" and "chilling."

Ambition doesn't mean money — it means direction.

2. They know who they are *becoming,* not just who they are today.

If the only plan is survival, there's no room for partnership.

3. They make decisions with their future self in mind.

Maturity is when today's choices protect tomorrow's peace.

4. They don't mock your goals or make you feel "too much" for dreaming.

A partner who doesn't support your growth is a trap, not a soulmate.

5. They don't expect you to shrink for their comfort.

If you have to dim to keep them, they're not for you.

6. They want stability, not chaos disguised as "I'm just living."

Unpredictability is not personality. It's unpreparedness.

7. They see relationships as *teamwork,* not *ownership.*

"Us" planning beats "me" winning.

8. They're not intimidated by the idea of responsibility.

Avoiding responsibility now turns into crisis later.

9. They're building something — even if it's small — that shows discipline.

Consistency over hype.

10. They don't need to know the final destination to walk with purpose.

Direction > perfection.

REFLECTION PROMPT

"If we stayed together, what would our lives look like in 5 years?"

BECOME THE GREEN FLAG

91. You apologize clearly.
92. You respect boundaries.
93. You communicate honestly.
94. You regulate emotions.
95. You walk away from disrespect.
96. You don't chase validation.
97. You choose growth over ego.
98. You don't entertain chaos.
99. You take accountability.
100. You align your standards with your behavior.

Bonus Chapter

When There Are Too Many People in the Relationship

A healthy relationship should involve two people making decisions together.

Not a committee.

But sometimes a relationship slowly becomes crowded with invisible voices.

You make a decision together. You talk things through. You agree on a plan. Everything seems settled. Then the person goes home. They talk to someone else.

Maybe it's their mother. Maybe it's a sister. Maybe it's a friend who has always had influence. Maybe it's someone they "used to date." Maybe it's the childhood friend who has always been around.

The next time you see them, something has changed. Their opinion changed. Their attitude changed. The plan changed.

What you agreed on yesterday is suddenly different today.

If this happens once in a while, it may simply mean someone needed time to think something through.

But when it happens over and over again, something else is going on.

Someone outside the relationship still has the power to override decisions made inside it.

And that creates instability.

Because you never really know if the agreement you made will still exist tomorrow.

When Relationships Become Group Projects

Some people grow up making decisions as a group. Their friends weigh in. Their family weighs in. Their siblings weigh in.

Everyone has an opinion about what they should do.

That pattern can follow them into dating.

Every disagreement becomes something they take back to the group. This means that they are discussing everything you two discuss with other people. Like, regularly.

Every decision gets filtered through someone else. Are you okay with that?

But it's a new day and instead of echoing what you two talked about yesterday, they are saying, "We decided."

We – yeah, that's us.

But they say:

"My mom thinks..."
"My sister said..."
"My friend told me..."

Don't get this wrong, advice from trusted people is normal. But when those voices begin steering the relationship, the partnership becomes unstable. Because now the relationship no longer belongs to the two people in it.

It belongs to whoever spoke to them last, even if that last person was the group chat.

The problem isn't the other people. Friends and family are not the problem. Everyone has people they trust. The problem is when someone believes those voices should control their relationship decisions.

Some people truly think this is normal.

They believe:

- their friends should help decide how serious the relationship is
- their family should weigh in on every disagreement
- their group should influence how they treat you

You might even hear things like:

"Bros before relationships."

"My mom says you're doing too much."

"My sister thinks you're wrong."

At that point, the relationship isn't really between two people anymore. It's a committee meeting, and committees don't build stable relationships.

A Simple Reality

If every decision you make together can be overturned by someone else later, you are not actually part of the decision.

Healthy relationships require two people who can:

- think for themselves
- make decisions together
- stand by those decisions

Advice can exist. Influence will always exist. But the final responsibility should stay with the two people in the relationship, not the group.

DATE THIS / NOT THAT

☑ Date This:

Thinks things through before agreeing and stands by decisions once they're made. *(Translation: My decisions aren't easily overturned by outside voices.)*

✕ Not That:

Agrees with you, then disappears and returns with a completely different decision. *(Translation: Someone else is helping decide the relationship.)*

☑ DATE THIS:

"I respect my family's opinion, but the decision is ours." *(Translation: Advice is welcome, but the relationship belongs to us.)*

✕ Not That:

"My mom said we should do something different." *(Translation: Someone outside the relationship has veto power.)*

Date This:

"I value my friends, but I make my own relationship decisions." *(Translation: I'm responsible for how I show up in my relationships.)*

Not That:

"My friends said I shouldn't take this too serious." *(Translation: My friends help decide how I treat you.)*

REFLECTION

Have you ever felt like someone else had more influence over your relationship than you did? Think honestly about that experience.

Healthy relationships require two people who can make decisions together — without the group running the conversation.

Learning to recognize green flags in other people is important. But there's another step that matters just as much.

The healthiest relationships happen when both people bring maturity, independence, and self-awareness into the partnership.

That means being able to make decisions, set boundaries, and take responsibility for your own behavior — without needing a crowd to guide you.

In the next chapter, we turn the focus inward. Because the goal isn't just to find green flags in someone else.

It's to *become* one.

CHAPTER 10

BECOME THE GREEN FLAG

You don't attract what you deserve — you attract what you're aligned with.

It's easy to make a list of what you want in someone else.
It's harder — but way more powerful — to become the kind of person who could *actually thrive* in a healthy relationship.

The truth is:

If you're used to chaos, peace will feel "boring."
If you're used to fixing, healthy will feel "too easy."
If you're used to chasing, consistency will feel "one-sided."
If you're unhealed, red flags will feel familiar — and familiarity feels like chemistry.

You don't need to be perfect to deserve love.
You just need to be **growing in the same direction you want to receive.**

It is easy to make a list. Harder to become the standard. You cannot demand maturity while avoiding growth. You cannot ask for loyalty while entertaining instability.

You cannot expect safety while creating chaos. The healthiest relationships form between two people committed to development.

Not perfection. Growth.

What Direction Looks Like

- They have goals, even if modest.
- They take responsibility for their progress.
- They think about the future.
- They value stability.
- They support your growth instead of competing with it.

Direction is not perfection. It is intention.

Natalie (Girl's POV)

At 19:

Natalie loved that he was relaxed. He didn't stress. He didn't overthink. He "went with the flow."

But he also had no plan. No ambition. No urgency to grow. She thought love would motivate him.

Love cannot replace drive.

Reece (Guy's POV)

At 22:

Reece admired her confidence. She talked about dreams constantly. But she never took steps toward them. He realized something important: Talking about success is not the same as building it.

FAST FORWARD — Age 33

Natalie is raising a child with someone who is still "figuring it out."

Reece is building a life with someone who had direction long before he arrived.

Potential without discipline becomes stagnation.

DATE THIS / NOT THAT — Self Edition

✅ **Date This:**

"I'm working on becoming the kind of person my future partner will feel safe with." (Translation: I build the qualities I want in someone else.)

❌ **Not That:**

"I want someone loyal, healed, patient, respectful, and mature."
...while still being inconsistent, reactive, insecure, and unwilling to grow.
(Translation: I expect someone else to be what I'm not willing to become.)

✅ **Date This:**

"I'm learning how to recognize healthy people — and become one."
(Translation: I take responsibility for the patterns I participate in.)

❌ **Not That:**

"I keep attracting the wrong people."
(Translation: I'm blaming patterns instead of examining my choices.)

✅ **Date This:**

"I'm building a life that a healthy relationship could fit into."
(Translation: A relationship should add to my life, not rescue it.)

❌ **Not That:**

"I just want someone who will fix my life."

(Translation: I expect a relationship to solve problems I won't face myself.)

The Truth

Choose someone whose present actions match their future words. You deserve a partner — not a project.

Why This Matters

You attract what feels familiar. If chaos feels normal, peace will feel strange. If drama feels exciting, stability will feel dull.

You must train yourself to recognize calm as valuable. You must train yourself to become calm.

Maria (Girl's POV)

At 17:

Maria used to think being "ride or die" meant loving people through everything — lies, disrespect, cheating, chaos.

By 25, she realized the problem wasn't just who she chose — it was that she kept abandoning herself to prove she was "loyal."

She finally learned: **Healthy girls don't ride or die — they stand, walk away, /or build with someone who walks with them.**

Jay (Guy's POV)

At 20:

Jay used to think being a "gentleman" meant picking girls who needed fixing, saving, or rescuing. Then he realized he was choosing brokenness because *he wanted to feel needed* — not because the relationship was healthy.

At 30, he says:
A healed man doesn't look for a damsel — he looks for a partner.

FAST FORWARD (Age 35)

Maria is now married to a man who loves her *without needing her to shrink or suffer first.* Her peace came when she stopped trying to be "the exception" and started being *the standard.*

Jay is raising daughters who will never have to wonder what respect looks like. He didn't just find a green flag — he became one first.

When you become the peace, you stop craving the chaos.

Good love isn't rare.
Unhealed eyes just can't recognize it yet.

---

10 GREEN FLAGS IN *YOU*

1. You don't punish people for being honest.

Safety invites truth. Threat invites lies.

2. You can apologize without making it a performance.

Mature love says: "You're right. Let me fix that."

3. You don't require someone else to regulate your emotions.

Love is support — not emotional babysitting.

4. You can feel attraction without losing self-respect.

The more you value yourself, the slower you give access.

5. You don't chase attention — you build value.

People who know their worth don't beg for confirmation.

6. You don't call loyalty "clingy" and distance "freedom."

Love is not a prison. It's a partnership.

7. You can walk away from what breaks you, even if you're attached.

Healing starts when self-respect is louder than fear.

8. You don't use people to fix loneliness or insecurity.

Real connection requires fullness, not desperation.

9. You don't blame "how you were raised" for hurting people.

Growth is a choice, not an accident.

10. You don't ask for what you're not willing to give.

The standard you set for others should be the one you live too.

What Becoming the Green Flag Looks Like

- You apologize without defensiveness.
- You respect boundaries.
- You regulate your emotions.
- You communicate clearly.
- You walk away from disrespect.
- You value growth.
- You choose integrity over ego.

You do not need to be flawless.

You need to be accountable.

The Final Truth

You do not control who approaches you.

You control who you choose.

The future version of you is shaped by the decisions you make now.

Choose with wisdom.

FINAL REFLECTION PROMPT

1. What kind of person do I want to be in someone's life?

CONCLUSION

CHOOSE WITH THE FUTURE IN MIND

At 18, everything feels immediate.

At 30, everything feels cumulative.

The small things you overlook now become patterns later. The boundaries you ignore now become expectations later.

The disrespect you tolerate now becomes the tone of your home later. You do not have to fear relationships.

You simply need to recognize what is safe. Healthy love exists. But it requires clarity. And clarity requires courage. Choose with the future in mind.

Appendix A : Master List of 100 Green Flags:

💚 100 GREEN FLAGS

CHAPTER 1 — RESPECT (1–10)

1. Listens without interrupting.
2. Respects your "no" the first time.
3. Doesn't joke at your expense.
4. Speaks respectfully even when upset.
5. Treats you the same in public and private.
6. Doesn't pressure your boundaries.
7. Doesn't flirt to make you insecure.
8. Values your opinions.
9. Doesn't compete with your confidence.
10. Treats everyone with dignity, not just you.

CHAPTER 2 — COMMUNICATION (11–20)

11. Says what they mean clearly.
12. Doesn’t disappear without explanation.
13. Can apologize without blaming you.
14. Doesn’t mock your feelings.
15. Clarifies misunderstandings calmly.
16. Doesn’t expect mind-reading.
17. Can handle hard conversations.
18. Keeps tone respectful during disagreement.
19. Doesn’t gaslight or minimize concerns.
20. Makes you feel calm, not anxious.

CHAPTER 3 — CONSISTENCY (21–30)

21. Follows through on promises.
22. Shows up when they say they will.
23. Doesn’t love-bomb then withdraw.
24. Is steady over time.
25. Doesn’t “switch up” after getting comfortable.

26. Doesn't only show effort when losing access.
27. Doesn't punish with silence.
28. Is reliable with time and plans.
29. Doesn't make you compete for attention.
30. Cares consistently, not conditionally.

CHAPTER 4 — EMOTIONAL MATURITY (31–40)

31. Owns mistakes without excuses.
32. Regulates anger.
33. Doesn't threaten breakup during conflict.
34. Doesn't guilt-trip.
35. Doesn't weaponize trauma.
36. Takes responsibility for growth.
37. Doesn't blame their past for bad behavior.
38. Can disagree respectfully.
39. Handles stress without lashing out.
40. Values growth over ego.

CHAPTER 5 — CHARACTER (41–50)

41. Is honest even when it costs them.
42. Keeps promises.
43. Shows humility.
44. Speaks well of others.
45. Doesn't gossip excessively.
46. Respects people who can't benefit them.
47. Doesn't brag about basic decency.
48. Celebrates your wins.
49. Has integrity when unobserved.
50. Doesn't manipulate to get their way.

CHAPTER 6 — SOCIAL MEDIA (51–60)

51. Online behavior matches real-life values.
52. Doesn't act single online.
53. Doesn't entertain flirtatious comments.
54. Doesn't hide you to appear available.
55. Doesn't DM others secretly.
56. Doesn't subtweet you.
57. Doesn't seek validation excessively.

58. Doesn't embarrass exes publicly.
59. Is transparent about digital boundaries.
60. Protects your dignity online.

CHAPTER 7 — CONFLICT (61–70)

61. Doesn't insult during arguments.
62. Doesn't raise voice to dominate.
63. Doesn't block or ghost as punishment.
64. Doesn't threaten to leave to gain control.
65. Seeks resolution, not victory.
66. Apologizes sincerely.
67. Doesn't bring up past issues to win.
68. Doesn't humiliate you publicly.
69. Communicates during cooling-off periods.
70. Makes you feel safe after conflict.

CHAPTER 8 — PACE & PRESSURE (71–80)

71. Moves at a healthy pace.

72. Doesn't rush exclusivity.
73. Doesn't rush physical intimacy.
74. Doesn't isolate you from friends/family.
75. Doesn't pressure long-term decisions quickly.
76. Builds trust before labels.
77. Is patient with your comfort level.
78. Doesn't guilt you for boundaries.
79. Doesn't love-bomb to secure loyalty.
80. Lets the relationship develop naturally.

CHAPTER 9 — DIRECTION (81–90)

81. Has clear goals.
82. Works toward self-improvement.
83. Values stability.
84. Supports your ambitions.
85. Doesn't feel threatened by your success.
86. Makes responsible life decisions.
87. Has discipline.
88. Doesn't rely on fantasy plans.

89. Thinks long-term.
90. Wants partnership, not dependency.

CHAPTER 10 — BECOMING THE GREEN FLAG (91–100)

91. You apologize clearly.
92. You respect boundaries.
93. You communicate honestly.
94. You regulate emotions.
95. You walk away from disrespect.
96. You don't chase validation.
97. You choose growth over ego.
98. You don't entertain chaos.
99. You take accountability.
100. You align your standards with your behavior.

Keep Learning

This book focused on **green flags** — the signs of healthy relationships. There is a workbook that goes with this book.

If you want to understand the other side of the picture, the **200 Red Flags series** explores the warning signs that often appear before relationships become toxic or unstable. Knowing both helps you make wiser choices.

...from the 200 Red Flags Series

- Apologies that never lead to change
- Sudden personality shifts after commitment
- Jealousy disguised as protection
- Public charm, private disrespect
- Constant crisis used as control

Red Flags: The Track Is Not Safe (book & workbook)

Other Relationship Books by Dr. Marlene Miles:

Already Married in the Spirit: ***Why You May Not Be Married in the Natural*** https://a.co/d/gVSzfQ2

Anti-Marriage, ***The Spirit of*** https://a.co/d/fEKrHFu

Too Many Wives: ***Why You Have Lady Problems***

Unbreak My Heart: ***Don't Let Me Die***

Why Do I Keep Meeting the Same Guy?

https://a.co/d/0BcAWmW

SOUL TIE book. Soul Tie Workbook. Soul Tie Prayer Manual

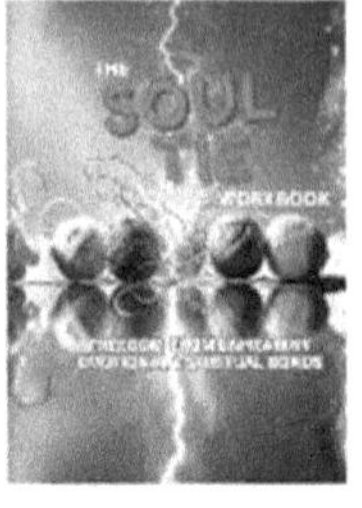

Players Gonna Play

Second Marriage, Third--, *Any Marriage*

https://a.co/d/6m6GN4N

Seducing Spirits: Idolatry & Whoredoms

https://a.co/d/4Jq4WEs

Six Men Short: What Has Happened to all the Men?

We Get Along, Right? Compatibility for Couples – (book & workbook)

About the Author

Dr. Marlene Miles writes about relationships, discernment, and personal development. Her work focuses on helping readers recognize healthy patterns, establish strong boundaries, and make wiser decisions in their personal lives.

Through books and teaching, she aims to give people practical tools for understanding behavior, protecting their peace, and building relationships rooted in respect and maturity.

Thank you for acquiring and reading these books, I hope they've made a difference in your life.

www.ingramcontent.com/pod-product-compliance
Lightning Source LLC
LaVergne TN
LVHW011030110826
845149LV00015B/3356
* 9 7 8 1 9 7 1 9 3 3 3 7 5 *